I Wish I Could Go to . . .

by Mrs. MacNeil's class
with Tony Stead

capstone

Introduction

by Mrs. MacNeil's class

Our state is Michigan, and it is a great place to live or visit. There is so much to see and do, but the beauty of Michigan is its best quality. Did you know that it is the only state that touches four of the five Great Lakes? No matter where you are in Michigan, you are never more than a few hours away from one of the lakes. In addition to this, Michigan has beautiful beaches, majestic sand dunes, lush forests, and fertile farmlands.

Michigan is not only beautiful but interesting, too. There are many places to visit, such as Mackinac Island, Pictured Rocks, Sleeping Bear Dunes, and Tahquamenon Falls. However, there are many historical places to visit as well. Greenfield Village in Dearborn is one of our favorites because it not only has a historical museum but it also has a village that you can tour to see how Americans worked and lived in the past.

Michigan is well known for its production of motor vehicles and the production line, which is a mechanical system in a factory where a product is moved through stages. Many food brands are also produced in Michigan.

Michigan is a great place to live, and we encourage everyone to visit. However, for those of us who have lived here most of our lives, we wanted to find other places of interest to visit. So our class did some research on other states and countries, and we found many places we wish we could go to!

Texas

by Michael

One state I would love to visit is the Lone Star State: Texas! The reason I chose Texas is because I would like to see Austin, Texas, the state capital. Did you know it is the 11th largest city in the United States? There are other interesting places in Texas that would be amazing to see as well.

Texas has many big cities like Dallas, San Antonio, Houston, and Austin. They also have interesting facts about them. For instance, Austin was founded in 1839. Dallas was founded in 1841. Dallas's nickname is the Big D.

Texas has many landmarks like SeaWorld, San Antonio Zoo, Gravity Amusement Park, Houston Zoo, Palo Duro Canyon, and Alamo Mission in San Antonio. Palo Duro Canyon has amazing things to see, such as prairie dogs and the Red River.

There are different kinds of industries in Texas, such as steel, banking, farming, oil, and computers. The farming industry in Texas involves livestock farming and growing cotton and other crops. The Texas steel industries make a variety of products, such as pipelines, bridges, household items, and cars.

From big cities to amusement parks, Texas has it all. I think Texas is the best state in the whole world!

Map of Texas

State Flag

State Flower
Blue
Bonnett

Amarillo

Palo Duro
Canyon

Ben Hogan
Died

Fort Worth

Stephenville
Ben Hogan
Was Born

Austin

Sea
World

Alamo
Mission

San Antonio

Dallas
Cowboys

Zero
Gravity
Amusment
Park

Dallas

Houston

Houston
Zoo

Houston
Texans

Six Flags
Fiesta

New York

by Anna

Temples, castles, big cities, jungles. If I could travel anywhere in the world, where would I go? I would choose to visit the state of New York! There is so much to do that I have already planned this trip.

The Big Apple, which is the nickname of New York City, is huge and exciting. There is so much to see and do like going to Central Park or maybe the Bronx Zoo. The Bronx Zoo would be my first stop. I really want to see the food stop called the Dancing Crane Café. In addition to the zoo, I would visit the American Museum of Natural History.

While on my trip, I'd want to see other big cities in the state. Buffalo is the second biggest city. Once a national magazine named Buffalo the third best food city in the world because of the chicken wings. People say Buffalo wings are cooked to perfection! I would like to try those while I'm there.

If I visit New York in the spring, I might hear the state bird singing! Some of New York's state symbols are the state flower (rose), the state tree (sugar maple), and the state bird (the eastern bluebird). The eastern bluebird was designated, or chosen, as the official state bird in 1970.

If I went to New York, I know I would have a lot of fun and learn interesting facts along the way. I already have a plan, and I am ready to go!

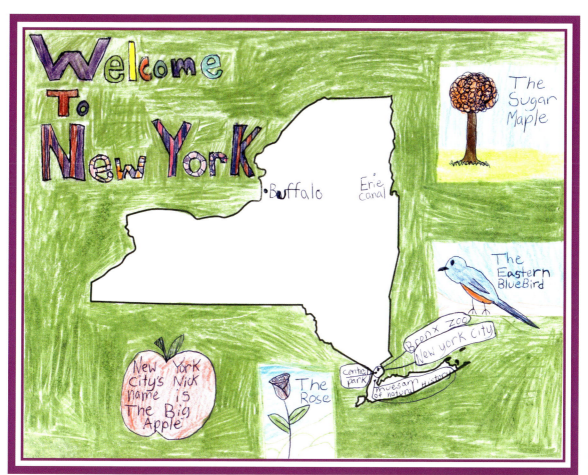

South Dakota

by Trever

If I could go anywhere, I would go to South Dakota. I would see the Crazy Horse Monument and Mount Rushmore. Did you know that the Crazy Horse Monument was made for an American Indian warrior? He went by the name Crazy Horse. Mount Rushmore has the faces of four U.S. presidents carved into it. But there's so much more to see in South Dakota.

South Dakota certainly has some beautiful landforms. One of them is the Rushmore Cave. Rushmore Cave is one of the closest caves to Mount Rushmore. It is the ninth longest cave in South Dakota and measures a distance of 3,652 feet.

Clearly South Dakota has a lot of great tourist attractions. It attracted people long ago, too. In the spring of 1876, miners and merchants flooded the area in search of gold.

South Dakota's biggest cities are Sioux Falls and Rapid City. Sioux Falls is on the east side of South Dakota. Rapid City is on the west side. It sits in the Black Hills.

Every year millions of people visit Rapid City and the Black Hills to see Mount Rushmore, Crazy Horse Monument, and much more! What would you like to see first if you were traveling to South Dakota?

Hawaii

by Cadence

If I could visit anywhere in the world, I would go to Hawaii. With fresh coconuts and pineapples to amazing waterfalls and landforms, there is so much there that is fun for family and friends.

Hawaii is a chain of islands in the Pacific Ocean. There are tons of places to go in Hawaii. But the island of Maui is my favorite. Rainbow Falls is one place you are going to want to see. In addition to the beauty, you get to see animals and exotic plants! And if you're thirsty, visit the Coconut Shack to watch coconuts get broken open just for you! They pick the sweetest ones. So you can get a nice sweet drink of coconut milk!

There are also many tourist attractions in Hawaii. One of my favorites is humpback whale watching in Lahaina Harbor.

Long ago people in Hawaii believed there was a living creature in the water that they called a sea serpent. Today they still tell legends about this creature. I can't wait to visit Hawaii so I can find out if it's really true!

Mississippi

by Brandon

The place I would love to visit is Mississippi. I have learned so much about Mississippi that I'd love to go and see all of the tourist attractions.

Mississippi is located in the United States below Tennessee and next to Alabama. Mississippi has big cities like Jackson and Gulfport. One fact about Jackson is that it has about 300 restaurants, many with authentic deep southern cooking. Jackson is Mississippi's largest city. The next largest city is Gulfport.

There are lots of landmarks in Mississippi. These include Elvis Presley's birthplace and museum, Natchez National Historical Park, Old Capitol Museum, and Tupelo National Battlefield. The battlefield is where General Nathan Forrest last commanded his confederate soldiers on horses to fight against the Union in the Battle of Tupelo on July 14–15, 1864.

One I place I would like to see is the Tupelo Automobile Museum. It has a timeline that shows how cars have changed over the years.

Overall Mississippi has a lot of tourist attractions and landmarks. Mississippi would be fun to visit because there are a lot of places to go and things to see.

This is Mississippi

Italy

by Ava

     If I could visit any state or country in the world, I would love to go to Italy because I would like to taste some of their famous Italian food. It would also be super cool to see the Leaning Tower of Pisa. Did you know that the Leaning Tower of Pisa weighs almost 16,000 tons?

     Italy is a country in Europe. Italy juts out like a boot into the Mediterranean Sea. Milan, Florence, Lake Garda, the Amalfi Coast, and the ruins of Pompeii are all great places to see, but the most interesting to me is the Leaning Tower of Pisa. The Leaning Tower of Pisa has 294 steps on the north side and 296 steps on the south side. The Leaning Tower started leaning because it was built on soil that couldn't hold its weight. Construction started on the tower in 1173 and started leaning in 1178.

Italy is also famous for its delicious Italian food. You can eat Italian food in America, but wouldn't you want to taste the real thing? Italy is known for their pasta, pizza, and gelato, or ice cream.

From a leaning tower to ruins to fabulous food, there are so many reasons to visit Italy. Don't you want to go?

Mexico

by Madisyn

If I could go anywhere in the world, I would go to the country of Mexico. I would love to visit Mexico because I want to learn the traditional dances. Mexico has famous dances that are easy to learn with few steps or hard to learn with many steps.

Mexico is on the continent North America. Major landforms in Mexico are mountains, plateaus, and plains. Mexico also has many big cities, but a really famous city is Mexico City. Did you know it is the capital of Mexico?

There are a lot of tourist attractions in Mexico, including landmarks like Copper Canyon. It is located in the state of Chihuahua in Mexico. Chichen Itza is another famous attraction. It is an ancient city built by the Mayan people. It is a very popular site for visitors in Mexico.

Map Of Mexico

Mexico has symbols that stand for it. The Mexican flag, the national anthem, and the coat of arms stand for the country. The coat of arms is important to Mexico because it is on the flag. Did you know that Mexico's coat of arms is a golden eagle standing on a cactus eating a snake?

There are many places in the world to visit. I would go to Mexico with all the things to do and see. But mostly I would like to learn the traditional dances and hear the music.

Ireland

by Whitney

From the country's mountains to the evergreen forests to the sandy shores, if I could go anywhere in the world, my destination would be the country of Ireland.

Dublin is Ireland's largest city. It is also the country's capital. People visit Dublin to see the Dublin Zoo and St. Patrick's Cathedral. The cathedral is the largest church in Ireland.

Another attraction is Blarney Castle in the county Cork of Ireland. At the top of the castle is the famous Blarney Stone. Tourists visit Blarney to kiss a famous stone! Legend says if you kiss the stone it will give you the gift of eloquence. Eloquence means a person can express himself or herself smoothly and clearly.

Ireland is a beautiful country with many places to visit. Do you want to kiss the Blarney Stone or go to the Dublin Zoo?

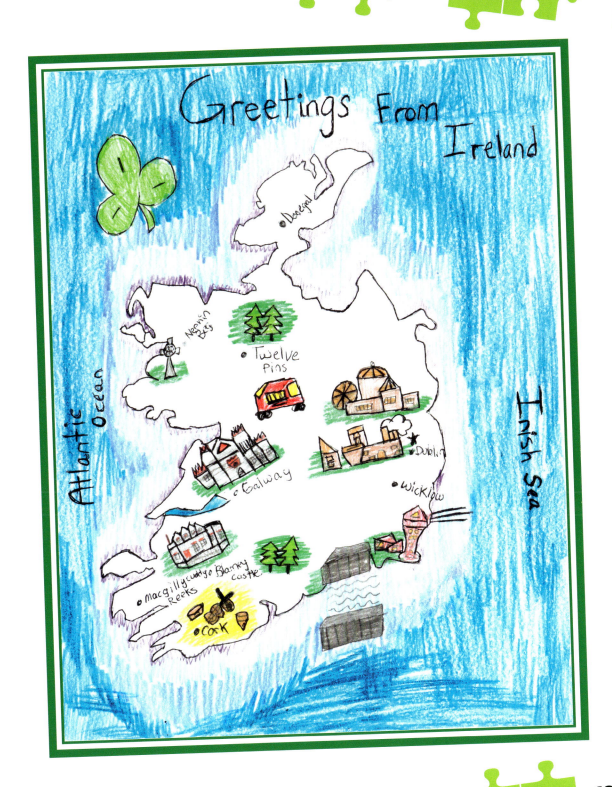

Germany

by Jaelynn

Out of any place in the world, I would go to Germany. I learned so much about the cities, landmarks, and events that I'd like to pack my bags and leave tomorrow.

The cities in Germany are amazing! Frankfurt is a big city in Germany. Did you know Frankfurt is one of Germany's oldest cities? Frankfurt is famous for the Frankfurter, which in America is a hot dog.

Aside from the food, there are many different castles in Germany visited by millions of people every year. For example, Heidelberg Castle, Albrechtsburg Castle, and Neuschwanstein Castle are some of the most popular ones.

After seeing the sites, it would be fun to go to a festival. Have you ever heard of Oktoberfest? Oktoberfest is one of the world's largest festivals and is held in Munich. It is a 16 daylong folk festival. More than 6 million people attend the event each year.

These are some of the reasons I want to go to Germany. I could see and do many things in this interesting country!

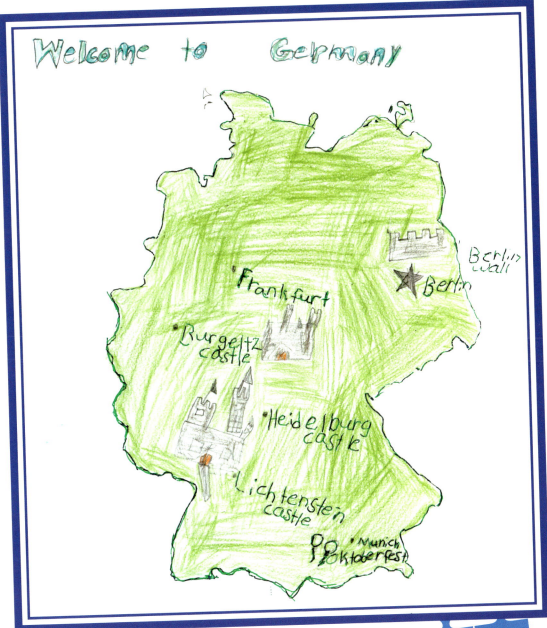

Spain

By Amari

One country I want to visit is Spain. I would see the beautiful flowers, visit water parks, jump into the ocean, and go to the lovely houses and palaces.

Did you know Madrid, Spain, is the third most populated city in Europe? It is the country's capital. Madrid is the most visited city in Spain. People visit its many museums, parks, and the Royal Palace.

Some landmarks in Spain are Barcelona's Sagrada Familia, Alcazar of Sevilla, Alhambra Palace, and the Canary Islands. The Sagrada Familia is an amazing structure that has been under construction since 1882. The Alhambra Palace is located in Granada, Spain. This fortress is made of red clay.

Spain has beautiful cities and fascinating landmarks. This is the country I would go to if I could visit anyplace.

Map of Spain

Park Guell

Alcazar of Segovia

Barcelona

Madrid
Royal Palace

Sagrada Familia Palace

Alcazar
of Sevilla

Alhambra
Palace

Siam
Park
Canary
Islands

Conclusion

Think about the title of the book. Where would you like to go? What makes that place so fascinating, and what would you like to see there?